Madam C. J. Walker

History
Maker
Bios

Susan Bivin Aller

BARNES & NOBLE

NEW YORK

The publisher thanks A'Lelia Bundles, Madam C. J. Walker's great-great-granddaughter and biographer, for her assistance with this book.

Text © 2007 by Susan Bivin Aller
Illustrations © 2007 by Lerner Publications Company

This 2007 edition published by Barnes & Noble, Inc.
by arrangement with Lerner Publications Company, a division of
Lerner Publishing Group, Minneapolis, MN.

Illustrations by Big Time Attic

Barnes & Noble, Inc.
122 Fifth Avenue
New York, NY 10011

ISBN-13: 978-0-7607-8195-1
ISBN-10: 0-7607-8195-8

Printed and bound in the United States of America

1 3 5 7 9 10 8 6 4 2

Mrs. Robertson

TABLE OF CONTENTS

INTRODUCTION

Sarah Breedlove Walker grew up in the South in the late 1800s. Slavery had ended in the United States. African Americans were free. But most black women like Sarah could get only low-paying jobs doing laundry and housework. Stress and poor health caused many of these women to have hair problems.

Sarah wanted a better life for her daughter and herself. So she invented products that helped black women's hair become healthy. She trained thousands of women to use and sell her products. Sarah became a millionaire. She helped other black women improve their lives, too, through education and hard work.

This is her story.

1 BORN FREE

A fireplace was the only source of heat in the Breedlove family's cabin in Louisiana. There, on December 23, 1867, Minerva Breedlove gave birth to her fifth child. Her other children had been born into slavery. But this little girl was born free. Minerva named her Sarah.

Sarah's parents had worked as slaves on a cotton plantation in Delta, Louisiana, for many years. But in the 1860s, terrible battles raged through the area. The U.S. Civil War (1861–1865) had begun. Sarah's parents left Delta with the plantation owners in 1862. They wanted to escape the fighting. While they were away, the U.S. government freed all people from slavery.

The families returned to Delta after the war ended. Sarah was born two years later. By that time, her parents had rented a small piece of land. They were growing cotton to make a living.

Sarah's first home was the Breedlove family's cabin in Delta, Louisiana.

When Sarah was old enough, she worked with her parents in the fields. She worked long hours picking cotton. Sarah and the other children found time for some fun, however. They caught crayfish in the bayous. They went to fish fries where people sang and danced. They attended church on Sundays with their families. Minerva twisted Sarah's hair into tight coils and tied them with strings. This kept her hair out of the way during work and play.

FREE BUT NOT EQUAL

On January 1, 1863, President Abraham Lincoln signed the Emancipation Proclamation. It granted freedom to slaves in the South. But their lives did not become better overnight. Few African Americans owned land or houses. Freed slaves could get only the lowest-paying jobs.

Young children picked cotton with adults when Sarah was a child.

Life changed for Sarah when she was about five years old. Her mother suddenly died. Less than two years later, her father died too. Sarah moved in with her married sister, Louvenia. But Louvenia's husband was not a nice man. He was often mean to Sarah.

In 1878, yellow fever broke out in the South. It killed more than three thousand people. Then the cotton crop failed. Sarah's family took the few things they owned and went to nearby Vicksburg, Mississippi, to look for work.

Louvenia's husband expected ten-year-old Sarah to find a job. He thought she should help bring in money for the family. Jobs doing laundry were always open to black women and girls. So Sarah became one of the many young black girls who picked up white people's laundry. She washed and ironed it and returned it a week later. Everything had to be scrubbed by hand on washboards. The strong soap stung Sarah's skin and eyes. She hauled heavy, wet laundry in and out of tubs filled with boiling water. Sometimes she burned herself on the hot irons.

Many African American girls and women did white people's laundry.

In 1889, more than 400,000 people lived in Saint Louis, Missouri. It was one of the biggest cities in the United States.

When she was fourteen, Sarah married a man named Moses McWilliams. "I married . . . in order to get a home of my own," she said later. She also wanted to get away from her sister's cruel husband. At seventeen, Sarah gave birth to her daughter, Lelia. Three years later, her husband died. Sarah wanted a better life for Lelia and herself. So in 1889, she traveled on a steamboat up the Mississippi River to Saint Louis, Missouri. Three of her brothers lived in Saint Louis. They worked as barbers in their own shop.

Sometimes Sarah and Lelia stayed with one of Sarah's brothers. Other times, they lived in rented rooms. Blacks and whites were segregated. They lived in separate neighborhoods. Some of the black neighborhoods were nice, but Sarah was too poor to live in them. Lelia and Sarah lived in dirty and dangerous places.

The only place where Sarah felt safe and cared for was at church. Women at the large Saint Paul African Methodist Episcopal (AME) Church welcomed Sarah. They reached out to her and to other newcomers.

SEGREGATION

African Americans were segregated. They were not allowed to go to white schools or stay in most hotels. They could not eat in restaurants or even use restrooms that were reserved for white people.

Sarah felt safe at the Saint Paul AME Church in Saint Louis.

In church, Sarah found the strength to keep going. She prayed for good things to happen in her life. But it was a long, hard road. She continued to support Lelia and herself by washing other people's laundry. Every day, Sarah sweated over the steaming tubs, her hair tightly covered by a scarf.

2 TAKING CHARGE

At church, Sarah met black women who were educated and well off. They believed that "thrift, self-help, charity, and education" would lift women like Sarah out of poverty. They helped Sarah enroll four-year-old Lelia in school. Sarah could barely read and write. She wanted Lelia to have the best education.

African Americans pose for a photo at their church. Churches were important meeting places in the late 1800s.

In 1894, when Sarah was twenty-six, she remarried. She hoped this man would be a good husband and father. But he was the wrong choice. He drank, couldn't hold a job for long, and abused her. Sarah already had a hard time supporting Lelia and herself on her earnings. She could not support him too. The marriage ended.

Meanwhile, Sarah's hair began to fall out. It left bald spots. Sarah's hair embarrassed her. She couldn't make herself look respectable for the people she wanted to impress.

Sarah's hair problems were not unusual among poor, black women. They worked long hours. So they didn't have much time to care for their hair. Their diets often did not have enough nutrients. And many could not afford safe hair treatments. All of these problems caused hair loss.

BAD HAIR DAYS

African American slaves had no time to fix their hair the way their ancestors in Africa had done. In slavery, they did not have combs, herbs, and sweet oils to make their hair beautiful. Instead, they used cornmeal and kerosene to clean their scalps. They pulled out knots with rough combs used for sheep's wool. And they oiled their hair with butter or bacon grease. When they tried to straighten their hair, they spread a mix of potatoes and lye on it. Lye was a strong substance used in making soap. The mixture burned their scalps.

Lelia Walker

Lelia grew into a lovely teenager. She was nearly six feet tall. She always dressed neatly in clean clothes that her mother had starched and ironed. Sarah wanted to get Lelia away from the crime and poverty in their neighborhood. She worked hard and saved enough money to send Lelia to a school for the children of former slaves.

At Saint Paul AME Church, Sarah developed a talent for organizing projects. She raised money to help others. She enjoyed being a leader. In a night school class for black women, Sarah learned to read and write.

Sarah was not happy with her hair.

Sarah desperately wanted to improve her appearance. She was ashamed of her short, dry, tangled hair. She saw ads for hair products for black women. The companies that made the products were almost always owned by white men. The ads told black women they should straighten their hair. Then they would look more like white women. Sarah didn't care about making herself look like a white woman. She just wanted her hair to be healthy and well groomed.

One day, Sarah heard of a black woman named Annie Pope-Turnbo. Annie made hair and scalp products. Sarah started using them. Her scalp became healthier. Her hair grew longer and didn't break off. She was so impressed that she became a sales agent, selling Pope-Turnbo products to other people. Soon she made more money in a week than she had made in two weeks doing laundry. "I got my start by giving myself a start," Sarah said proudly.

3 GROWING HAIR

Selling hair and scalp treatments brought Sarah more than money. It brought her hope that she could leave her washtubs behind. Sarah had only a limited education to help her succeed. But she had plenty of ambition and a good product that women needed.

Sarah sold Pope-Turnbo products in Saint Louis for two years. Then she was ready for the next step. In 1905, she moved to Denver, Colorado, to live with her sister-in-law. Sarah heard that the air was very dry in Denver. So women's hair was especially dry and brittle there. She wanted to tap into that big, new market. In a black newspaper, Sarah advertised herself as a hair and scalp specialist. Her ad stated that "Mrs. McWilliams, formerly of St. Louis, has special rates for a month to demonstrate her ability to grow hair."

*In the early 1900s, trains brought people to Denver Union Station. Its gateway (*BELOW*) welcomed visitors to Denver.*

At some point, Sarah figured out how to make her own hair and scalp treatments. She may have asked a drugstore worker or chemist to help her. Products such as the ones she was selling had been around for a long time. They usually contained the mineral sulfur to heal the scalp, as well as soothing oils, gels, beeswax, and perfume. Sarah could mix those ingredients at home. Why should she continue to sell Pope-Turnbo's products when she could make and sell her own?

Sarah may have gotten some of her ideas at E. L. Scholtz's pharmacy in Denver (BELOW). She worked there briefly.

Sarah worked hard to make good hair care products.

If a chemist helped Sarah develop her scalp treatment, Sarah never told anyone. "One night I had a dream," Sarah declared. "A big black man appeared to me and told me what to mix. . . . Some of the remedy was from Africa. . . . [I] put it on my scalp and in a few weeks my hair was coming in faster than it had ever fallen out."

Sarah's friend Charles J. Walker helped with her advertisements. She had known C. J. for several years in Saint Louis. He was good looking and stylish, and he seemed educated. He had worked on newspapers and in barber shops and bars. He thought of himself as a good salesman. C. J. impressed Sarah. In January 1906, Sarah married C. J. Walker.

Sarah started calling herself Madam C. J. Walker. "Madam" was a French word that hairdressers in those days often used as their title. It gave customers the feeling that someone of high class was serving them. Using her husband's initials instead of her own first name was also a mark of wealth and respect.

Sarah used her married name, Madam C. J. Walker, on her products.

Sarah before using her hair grower (CENTER) and after (LEFT AND RIGHT)

    In July 1906, ads for Madam Walker's Wonderful Hair Grower appeared in one of Denver's newspapers for African Americans. The ads showed pictures of Sarah before and after using her hair grower. In the before picture, Sarah had short, frizzy hair. In the after picture, she had long, healthy hair down to her shoulders.

Sarah and C. J. traveled around the South to promote her business. In each town they visited, they stayed in a rooming house. Customers could go there for scalp treatments. The Walkers introduced themselves to people at the town's black churches and social clubs. Then they demonstrated Sarah's products in a church or lodge hall. After that, they held training classes. Women learned how to use Walker products and become sales agents for the Wonderful Hair Grower. Lelia stayed in Denver to make the hair grower, soap, and oils.

Sarah demonstrates how to comb a woman's hair.

MORE THAN HAIR

Walker agents learned how to make their customers feel beautiful. "To be beautiful," Madam Walker said, "does not refer alone to the arrangement of the hair [or to] the perfection of the [skin]. . . . One must combine these qualities with a beautiful mind and soul." She insisted that her agents be good examples of cleanliness and loveliness when they gave hair treatments.

Madam Walker's business grew fast. Sarah earned as much money in two years as she had earned in her whole life. In 1908, she and C. J. moved to Pittsburgh, Pennsylvania. Sarah opened the Lelia College of Beauty Culture to train sales agents. African American women in Pittsburgh had few job choices. Most worked as maids or servants. Becoming Walker agents gave black women a chance to be independent and earn a good living.

The Walkers moved to Indianapolis, Indiana, in 1910. They decided it was a good place for black businesses. They bought land and made plans to build a headquarters and factory for the Madam C. J. Walker Manufacturing Company. Later that year, Sarah attended the conference of the National Association of Colored Women. She made a good impression on the people there. She wore fashionable clothes and swept her thick hair back in a stylish hairdo. She was the most successful businesswoman there.

4 BUSINESS SUCCESS

Sarah rented out rooms in her house to earn money for her growing company. Few hotels at that time accepted black guests. Sarah's house had fine furnishings, central heating, and home-cooked meals. Sarah did all the cooking. She also mixed hair preparations and gave hair treatments. At night, she did all the laundry. She worked hard to leave her old life behind.

Sarah's picture is on this box of her Wonderful Hair Grower.

Sarah looked for expert advice on how to develop her business. C. J. did not have enough business experience to help her. So she hired two young black lawyers. They gave her legal advice and managed her money. With their help, the Madam C. J. Walker Company became a national business. It had agents from coast to coast.

Sarah put herself at the center of marketing. She was a good speaker. Her lectures and demonstrations always drew crowds. She printed her picture on every Walker product. Newspapers told her story and kept the public aware of each step in her progress. Most people didn't know that Sarah had written many of the articles. She was becoming a celebrity.

In August of 1912, Sarah attended the convention of the National Negro Business League (NNBL). Her driver took her to Chicago in her fancy new convertible. Sarah made a dramatic entrance. She had on a wool dress, gloves, and high-buttoned shoes. She wore a large feathered hat on top of her thick head of hair.

Sarah hoped the man in charge of the convention, Booker T. Washington, would let her speak. He was the most respected black leader of the day. But he ignored her request to be put on the program.

Booker T. Washington (SEATED, SECOND FROM LEFT) was a member of the committee that led the National Negro Business League.

31

On the final day of the convention, Sarah stood and demanded to be heard. "Surely you are not going to shut the door in my face," she said to Washington. The audience turned to look at Sarah.

By 1912, Sarah (DRIVING) owned nice cars. She also wore fine, expensive clothing and hats.

"I feel that I am in a business that is a credit to the womanhood of our race," she continued. "I . . . came from the cotton fields of the South. I was promoted from there to the washtub. . . . From there I promoted myself into the business of [making] hair goods. . . . I know how to grow hair as well as I know how to grow cotton." The audience clapped and cheered her on.

"I have built my own factory on my own ground," Sarah proudly told them. "Now my [goal] in life is not simply to make money for myself. . . . I love to use a part of what I make in trying to help others."

Newspapers reported that Sarah's speech was one of the big hits of the conference. Her charm and the story of her success inspired all who heard her—all except Booker T. Washington. When Sarah finished, he made no comment. He just called on the next speaker.

Sarah's factory in Indianapolis, Indiana

Chicago was the biggest city Sarah had ever visited. In 1912, more than two million people lived in Chicago.

Sarah returned to Indianapolis after her triumph in Chicago. At home, she had another challenge to face. For some time, she and C. J. hadn't been getting along. He had started drinking too much. He was going out with other women. He had also revealed to others the secret formula for Sarah's hair grower. Sarah filed for divorce. C. J. begged her to give him some money. But Sarah stood firm. She would keep using his name for herself and the company, but she wouldn't give him a penny.

Sarah gave more and more large donations to charities. She gave the most to organizations that helped black people improve their lives. These included YMCAs, black schools and churches, and the National Association for the Advancement of Colored People. Sarah never forgot her long, difficult climb to reach success. She wanted to help make it easier for others. When people heard about her good works, her business grew even more.

Sarah gave money for the first YMCA for African American men in Indianapolis. In 1913, she and Booker T. Washington (SECOND AND THIRD FROM LEFT) attended its grand opening.

One year after Sarah's dramatic speech in Chicago, Booker T. Washington had changed his mind about her. He invited her to address the next NNBL convention in Philadelphia. She arrived in her new seven-passenger car. She was accompanied by her driver, an assistant, and Lelia. Sarah had been taking lessons in how to make speeches. She had also studied handwriting and proper manners. She was confident and elegant as she delivered a moving speech to the audience. Booker T. Washington called her "one of the most . . . successful businesswomen of our race."

5 GIVING HOPE

Sarah wanted the women in her family to lead the Walker Company. Lelia was next in line. But she had no children. So in 1912, Sarah helped Lelia adopt a thirteen-year-old girl named Mae Bryant. Mae was black but also had Native American and European ancestors. As a result, her hair was long, thick, and wavy. She became a stunning model for the Walker hair products. Sarah and Lelia educated Mae and trained her to take over the company one day.

Travel occupied much of Sarah's time each year. She spoke at churches and social club meetings across the United States and in the Caribbean. Women flocked to her lectures. She used a hand-operated projector to show pictures at her talks. She opened each lecture with a picture of the cabin where she was born. Then she showed pictures of successful black businesspeople. She also showed Madam Walker's hair care products and beauty salons. The last pictures showed her expensive cars and big, fancy homes.

Sarah stands in front of the Madam C. J. Walker College of Beauty Culture in Indianapolis.

Villa Lewaro

In 1918, Madam Walker built a grand house in Irvington-on-Hudson, New York. It was not far from where John D. Rockefeller and other wealthy people lived. She filled her house with furniture from around the world and planted Italian gardens. Sarah called her home Villa Lewaro. She said she had built it to show young black people "what a lone woman accomplished and to inspire them to do big things."

The message was clear. If Sarah could rise so high from poverty, so could others. And she could help them do it. She had made hairdressing into a respectable business, in which it was possible for women to earn a great deal of money.

In 1916, Sarah had an idea. Walker agents could work at colleges where most of the students were black. As "hair culturists," agents would provide hair care for students. Then they would train students to become Walker agents. More than twenty colleges accepted her offer within the first year.

Sarah continued to give money to institutions that helped African Americans. She spoke out on a number of political and social issues. She helped lead a protest to prevent violence against black people. She earned the same respect that Booker T. Washington, W. E. B. DuBois, James Weldon Johnson, and other black leaders had. She even went with others to see President Woodrow Wilson at the White House.

Villa Lewaro

Sarah loved to fill her home with beautiful furniture.

In 1919, Sarah traveled to Missouri to
introduce a new line of products. There,
she became very ill. She had been suffering
from kidney disease for several years. She
knew she had only a short time to live. "My
desire now is to do more than ever for my
race," she said. In her last days, she made
sure her great wealth would go to the
people she loved and the causes she
believed in. On May 25, 1919, Sarah died
at home in Irvington-on-Hudson, New
York. She was fifty-one.

Sarah Breedlove Walker raised herself up from the washtub by her own hard work. She wanted other black women to have the same chance to succeed. She taught them that hair care was not just about beauty. It was also about the pride and confidence they felt when their hair was well groomed.

By training women to become hair culturists, Sarah made it possible for thousands to leave dead-end jobs. She taught them how to become successful businesswomen. She taught them to imagine a better life for themselves—the way she had for herself years before.

TIMELINE

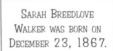
SARAH BREEDLOVE
WALKER WAS BORN ON
DECEMBER 23, 1867.

In the year . . .

1873? Sarah's mother died.

1875? her father died.   Age 7

1878 she moved with her older sister to Vicksburg, Mississippi.

1882 she married Moses McWilliams.   Age 14

1885 her daughter, Lelia, was born.

1888 Moses died.

1889 Sarah moved with Lelia to Saint Louis, Missouri.
she worked as a washerwoman.

1903 she used hair products made by Annie Pope-Turnbo.
Sarah worked as a Pope-Turnbo sales agent.

1905 she moved to Denver, Colorado.   Age 37
she invented her own hair products.

1906 she married Charles J. Walker.
Sarah began calling herself Madam C. J. Walker.

1908 she and C. J. moved to Pittsburgh, Pennsylvania.
she opened the first Lelia College.

1910 she moved to Indianapolis, Indiana.
she built a factory for the Madam C. J. Walker Manufacturing Company.

1912 she divorced C. J. Walker.

1913 Booker T. Washington invited her to speak at the NNBL conference.   Age 45

1918 she built Villa Lewaro.

1919 she died on May 25.   Age 51

44

THE COMPANY OF WOMEN

When Madam Walker died, her daughter, Lelia, became head of the Walker Company. But Lelia enjoyed social life more than business. She lived in a fancy house in Harlem, the New York City neighborhood where well-known black people gathered. Lelia was tall, beautifully dressed, charming, and generous. "She looked like a queen," someone reported. She donated money to musicians, actors, writers, and artists. She also held fabulous parties for them. Lelia died in 1931 at the age of forty-six.

Lelia's daughter, Mae Walker, ran the company until her death in 1945. The last family member in the company was Mae's daughter, A'Lelia Mae Perry, who died in 1976. The Walker Company was sold in 1986. A'Lelia Mae's daughter, A'Lelia P. Bundles, became a journalist. She wrote a biography of her great-great-grandmother, Madam C. J. Walker.

After Sarah died in 1919, her daughter, Lelia Walker, ran the Walker Company.

FURTHER READING

Bundles, A'Lelia Perry. *Madam C. J. Walker.* New York: Chelsea House, 1991. Madam Walker's great-great-granddaughter wrote this biography of her famous ancestor. It includes many historical photos.

Lasky, Kathryn. *Vision of Beauty: The Story of Sarah Breedlove Walker.* Cambridge, MA: Candlewick Press, 2000. Full-page color illustrations bring Madam Walker's story to life.

McKissack, Patricia, and Fredrick McKissack. *Madam C. J. Walker: Self-Made Millionaire.* Berkeley Heights, NJ: Enslow Publishers, 2001. This biography includes illustrations, black-and-white photographs, and a timeline.

Swain, Gwenyth. *A Hunger for Learning: A Story about Booker T. Washington.* Minneapolis: Millbrook Press, 2006. Read about the man Madam Walker admired so much. He worked his way up from slavery to become the most respected black educator in the country.

WEBSITES

Annie Turnbo Pope Malone
http://www.csupomona.edu/~plin/inventors/malone.html
This site tells the story of Annie Turnbo Pope Malone. Madam Walker sold Annie's products before creating her own. At that time, Annie called herself Annie Pope-Turnbo.

Bios of African Americans in History
http://www.enchantedlearning.com/history/us/aframer/
bios This page includes short biographies of many famous African Americans, including Madam Walker, Booker T. Washington, and W. E. B. DuBois.

The Official Website of Madam C. J. Walker
http://www.madamcjwalker.com This website is
maintained by Madam Walker's great-great-granddaughter
and biographer, A'Lelia Bundles.

SELECT BIBLIOGRAPHY

Bundles, A'Lelia. *On Her Own Ground: The Life and Times
of Madam C. J. Walker.* New York: Scribner, 2001.

Byrd, Ayana D., and Lori L. Tharps. *Hair Story: Untangling
the Roots of Black Hair in America.* New York: St. Martin's
Press, 2001.

Gates, Henry Louis, Jr., and Cornel West. *The African
American Century: How Black Americans Have Shaped
Our Country.* New York: Free Press, 2000.

O'Neil, William J., ed. *Business Leaders and Success: 55
Top Business Leaders and How They Achieved Greatness.*
New York: McGraw-Hill, 2004.

Peiss, Kathy. *Hope in a Jar: The Making of America's
Beauty Culture.* New York: Metropolitan Books, 1998.

Rooks, Noliwe M. *Hair Raising: Beauty, Culture, and
African American Women.* New Brunswick, NJ: Rutgers
University Press, 1996.

INDEX

Acknowledgments

For photographs and artwork: © A'Lelia Bundles/Walker Family Collection/ www.madamcjwalker.com, pp. 4, 7, 17, 18, 23, 25, 30, 33, 34, 39, 45; © Brown Brothers, pp. 9, 10; © Hulton Archive/Getty Images, p. 11; Used with permission of Documenting the American South, The University of North Carolina at Chapel Hill Libraries, p. 13; Library of Congress, pp. 15 (LC-USZ62-124830), 21 (LC-USZ62-107800), 24 (LC-DIG-ppmsca-02902), 31 (LC-DIG-ggbain-08329), 32 (LC-USZ62-88635) 35 (LC-USZ62-101148), 41 (HABS NY,60-IRV,5-1); The Denver Public Library, Western History Collection, Call # MCC-3904, p. 22; Indiana Historical Society, pp. 26 (both), 36, 42. **Front and back covers:** © A'Lelia Bundles/Walker Family Collection/ www.madamcjwalker.com.

For quoted material: pp. 11, 14, 19, 21, 23, 33, 34, 37, 39, 42, A'Lelia Bundles, *On Her Own Ground: The Life and Times of Madam C. J. Walker* (New York: Scribner, 2001); p. 26, A'Lelia Perry Bundles, *Madam C. J. Walker* (New York: Chelsea House, 1991).